All sorts of cats

What sort of cat would you choose? A fluffy Persian, a smooth Abyssinian or a chocolate-and-cream Siamese with unusual blue eyes? There are about 30 types of pedigree cats.

Even non-pedigree cats come in lots of different colours – white or black or ginger, often a mixture of all three. Tabby cats can have very beautiful markings, too.

Long-haired Persian

Ruddy Abyssinian

This Siamese kitten has pale blue eyes and a loud miaow. ▶

Good-looking cats

Soft fur, large eyes and long whiskers make a cat pretty to look at. But all these things help it to be a good hunter, too. A furry cat moves silently on soft paws.

Her large eyes adapt quickly to darkness or bright lights. Her whiskers are as long as the widest part of her body – if her whiskers go through a hole then the rest of her body can follow.

A Tortoiseshell British Shorthair washes its fur and whiskers.

6

A cat's pupils are narrow in daylight. After dark they widen to let in more light. ▶

Graceful movers

The hunting cat moves quickly and smoothly.
Cats can curl up tightly or stretch right out
because their skeletons are so flexible.

From a low, crouching position a cat can leap
on to a high wall or from one branch to another.
A cat nearly always makes a perfect landing,
even when it jumps from a great height.

An American Blue-cream Shorthair showing its sharp claws

A Tabby cat leaping from a tall tree to land gently on soft paws ▶

Eating

Wild cats eat their kill and then sleep for hours. Even tiny kittens can seem quite wild when they eat, sometimes growling fiercely to make sure no one steals their food.

Cats mainly eat meat and always need water to drink. They enjoy fish and milk, too. It is good for them to eat grass sometimes.

A Red Mackerel Tabby Persian crouching over its food

Cats will always choose a favourite place for curling up to sleep. ▶

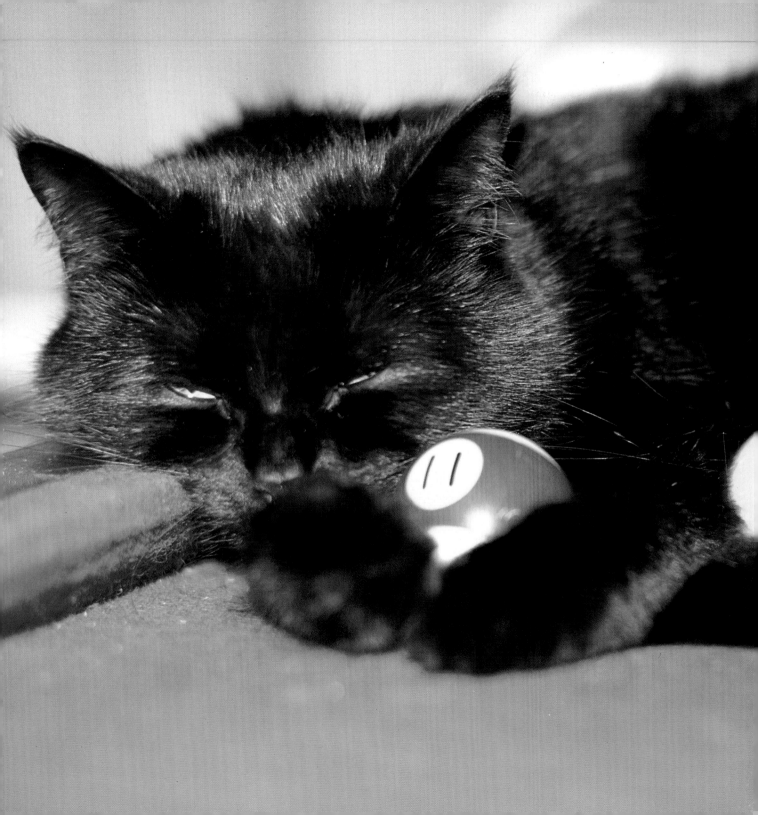

Cross cats

You can always tell when a cat is cross. A waving tail and flattened ears are warning signs. When a cat arches its back and makes its fur stick out, it is usually trying to scare off another cat or a dog.

Have you ever heard cats fighting? They hiss and yowl as they circle around each other, waiting for the moment to lash out with their claws.

The Red Burmese cat backs off from the Black one.

At only thirteen weeks old this Tabby kitten bravely displays its anger. ▶

The independent cat

Some cats love to be stroked and petted at any time, but others will be affectionate only when it suits them. Most cats will come when they are called at mealtimes, but usually they come and go as they please.

Cats like to find out things for themselves. They are always curious about a dripping tap or an open box. Sometimes their curiosity leads them into mischief.

This Blue Abyssinian obviously enjoys being stroked.

It's time for this curious Tabby to go and play somewhere else! ▶

Newborn kittens

A mother cat is pregnant for nine weeks. She looks for a quiet place to have her kittens. There are usually three or four kittens in a litter. Their ears are tiny and their eyes are tightly shut.

Kittens drink milk from their mother and sleep curled up against her. If the kittens are disturbed too often, the mother will carry them in her mouth to somewhere quieter.

A Tortoiseshell and White British Shorthair feeding her kittens

A mother cat carries the kitten by the scruff of its neck. ▶

Growing up

Kittens open their eyes about ten days after birth. Soon they can stagger to their feet. Small kittens, with their soft fur and stubby tails, are adorable, but they must be treated like babies, not like toys.

At six to eight weeks kittens are eating solid food and drinking from a saucer. Now they are old enough to leave home.

A little Tabby kitten at play is practising to be a hunter.

Kittens play-fighting their first battles against their brothers and sisters ▶

Handle with care

You should always be careful when handling a cat. If it doesn't want to be held it might scratch you. Always treat a cat with respect and remember that it has a mind of its own.

Approach a cat gently and hold it comfortably. Support the cat underneath and hold it firmly round the chest.

This little kitten feels well supported and secure.

A cat will usually warn you if it wants you to stay away. ▶

Know your cats

This chart will help you to recognise some of the different breeds of cats. A cat show is the best place to see them all.

Cats vary in shape, type of hair and colour. Different cats also have different natures. A Persian cat hates to be teased, but the Rex loves to play games. A Siamese can be noisy, but the Abyssinian is usually quiet.

Siamese

Angora

Rex

Burmese

Abyssinian

Tabby

Persian
Chinchilla

Colourpoint

British
Shorthair

Persian

Index

This edition published in 2003
©Aladdin Books Ltd 2003
Produced by
Aladdin Books Ltd
28 Percy Street
London W1T 2BZ

ISBN 0-7496-5405-8

First published in Great Britain in 1988 by
Aladdin Books/Watts Books
96 Leonard Street
London EC2A 4XD

Designer: Pete Bennett – PBD
Editor: Rebecca Pash
Illustrator: George Thompson
Picture Research: Cee Weston-Baker

Printed in UAE

Photographic credits:
Cover: PBD; pages 3, 5 7, 9, 13 & 15:
Bruce Coleman; page 11: Greg Evans;
pages 17 & 21: Spectrum; page 19: Sally
Anne Thompson/Animal Photgraphy